WHERE IS MY ? CONTINENT?

by Robin Nelson

first step nonfiction

Lerner Publications Company · Minneapolis

I live on a **continent**.

A continent is a big piece
of land.

Families live on continents
all around the world.

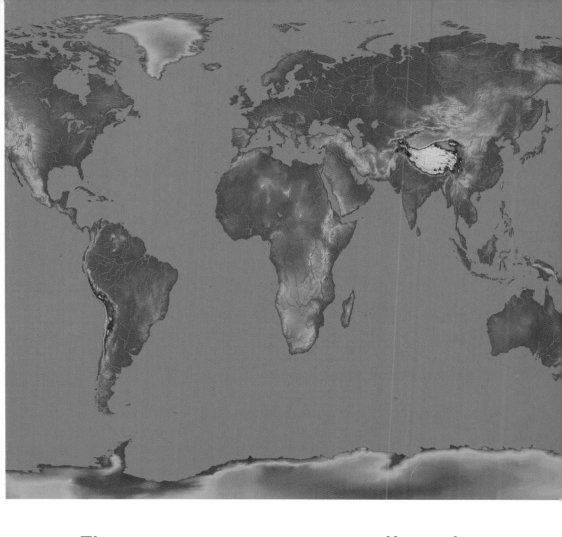

There are seven continents
on the earth.

I can find the continents on a **map.**

I can find the continents on
a **globe.**

Continents have water around them.

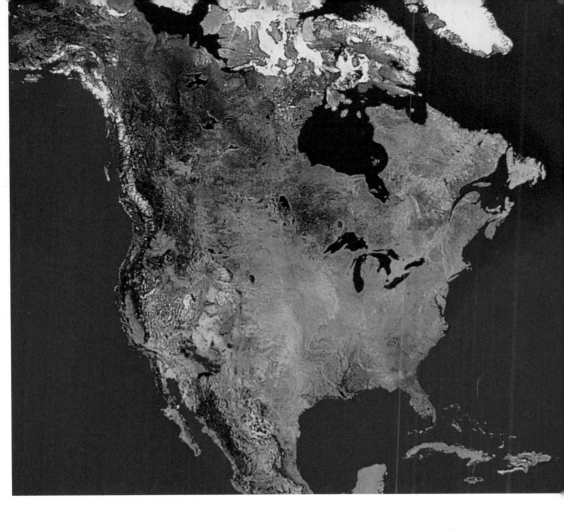

The continent I live on is called North America.

North America has the
Pacific Ocean on one side.

The Atlantic Ocean is on the other side.

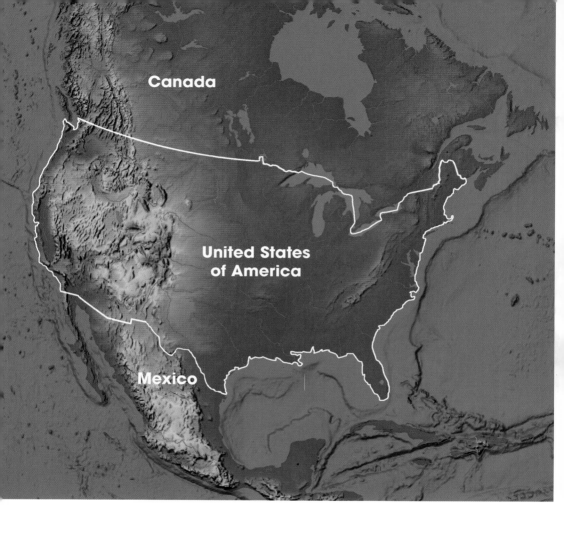

North America has three
large **countries**.

In North America, your
home can be by an ocean.

Your home can be in the mountains.

Your home can be on the **plains.**

Where is my continent?

My continent is on the earth,
where I live with my family.

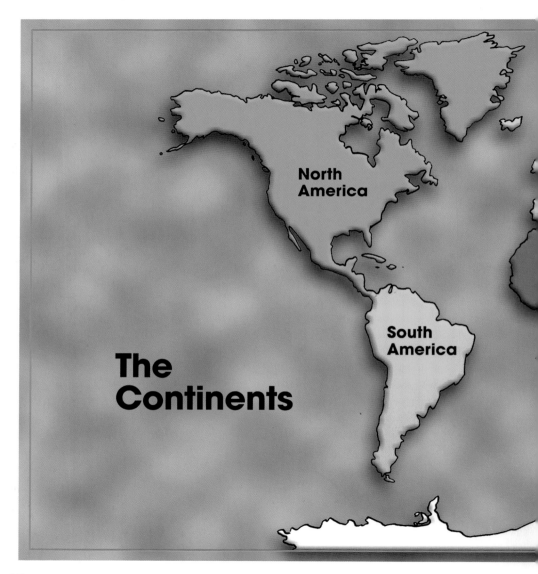

The
Continents

North
America

South
America

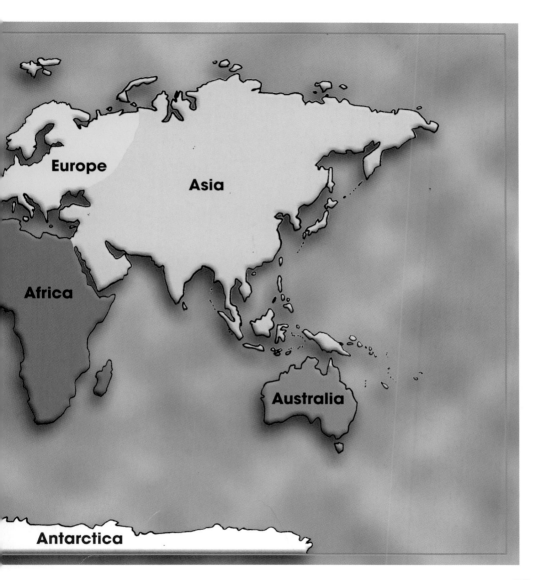

Europe

Asia

Africa

Australia

Antarctica

19

Continent Facts

 There are seven continents on the earth. They are Africa, Antarctica, Asia, Australia, Europe, North America, and South America.

At one time the seven continents were one huge continent.

Australia is the only continent that is also a country. It is the world's smallest continent. It is the largest island in the world.

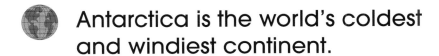 Antarctica is the world's coldest and windiest continent.

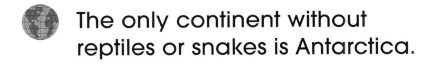 The only continent without reptiles or snakes is Antarctica.

 The Olympic symbol is made up of five rings, which stand for the continents of Europe, Asia, Africa, Australia, and North and South America.

More than 1,000 languages are spoken on the continent of Africa.

Glossary

 continent – one of the seven large landmasses of the earth

 countries – places where people live and share the same laws

 globe – a round model of the world

 map – a drawing of an area showing borders, towns, water, and mountains

 plains – large, flat areas of land

Index

The photographs in this book are reproduced through the courtesy of: © NASA, front cover, p. 8; © M. Bryan Ginsberg, p. 2; © Wolfgang Kaehler, pp. 3, 10, 16; © Sean Sprague/Photo Agora, p. 4; © Todd Strand/Independent Picture Service, p. 6, 22 (second from bottom); © Stockbyte, pp. 7, 22 (middle); © Earth Imaging/Stone, pp. 9, 22 (top); © Jeff Greenberg/Visuals Unlimited, pp. 11, 13; © Kent and Donna Dannen, p. 14; © Dick Poe/Visuals Unlimited, pp. 15, 22 (bottom); © Brooks Dodge/Photo Network, p. 17.

Lerner Publications Company
A division of Lerner Publishing Group, Inc.
241 First Avenue North
Minneapolis, MN 55401 U.S.A.

Website address: www.lernerbooks.com

Library of Congress Cataloging-in-Publication Data

Nelson, Robin, 1971–
    Where is my continent? / by Robin Nelson.
        p.   cm. — (First step nonfiction)
    Includes index.
    ISBN-13: 978–0–8225–0193–0 (lib. bdg. : alk. paper)
    ISBN-10: 0–8225–0193–7 (lib. bdg. : alk. paper)
    1. Continents—Juvenile literature. [1. Continents.]
    I. Title. II. Series.
    G133.N36 2002
    910'.02141—dc21   2001000959

Manufactured in the United States of America
6 7 8 9 10 11 – DP – 12 11 10 09 08 07